# MINIBEASTS

By
Robin Twiddy

FOREST
EXPLORER

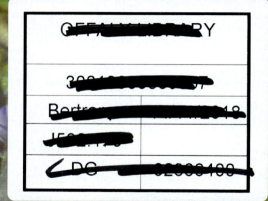

# BookLife
## PUBLISHING

©2018
BookLife Publishing
King's Lynn
Norfolk PE30 4LS

A catalogue record for this book is available from the British Library.

**ISBN:** 978-1-78637-476-9

**Written by:**
Robin Twiddy

**Edited by:**
Kirsty Holmes

**Designed by:**
Gareth Liddington

**Photocredits: All images are courtesy of Shutterstock.com.**

Cover – Fotofermer, hddigital, valzan, EtiAmmos, vvoe, anekoho, Subbotina Anna, PHUNTHEP SOMSANOI, 1 - suns07butterfly, 2 - EDPhotoZA 3 - Aleksandar Dickov, 4 - Patrick Foto, Smileus, 5 - Graham Taylor Photography, Kristina Shevchenko, horiyan, suriya yapin, 6 - hsagencia, Wanchai Orsuk, vnlit, Andrey Pavlov, 7 - IanRedding, chrom, 8 - Ger Bosma Photos, 9 - nujames10, 10 - kzww, Nikolay Antonov, 11 - Olha Insigh, 12 - Ivan Marjanovic, 13 - Yevhenii Chulovskyi, ivosar, 14 - Garmansheva Natalia, Pixel Memoirs, 15 - Hellen Grig, 16 - Vasilyev Alexandr, 17 - Ger Bosma Photos, Nikolay132, 18 - Hurst Photo, 19 - Brian A Jackson, 20 - Carlos Horta, 21 - sirtravelalot, 22 - frescomovie, Vector Tradition SM, saam3rd, MyraMyra, 23 - VarnaK, Samuel Borges Photography.

Images are courtesy of Shutterstock.com. With thanks to Getty Images, Thinkstock Photo and iStockphoto.

All facts, statistics, web addresses and URLs in this book were verified as valid and accurate at time of writing. No responsibility for any changes to external websites or references can be accepted by either the author or publisher.

# CONTENTS

Words that look like **this** can be found in the glossary on page 24.

# LET'S EXPLORE

## WELCOME, FOREST EXPLORER!
Today we will be looking for minibeasts in the forest. We will learn where they can be found, how they live and more.

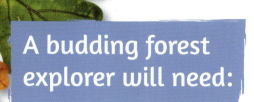
A budding forest explorer will need:

# GRAB YOUR EQUIPMENT

Magnifying Glass

Jar with Holes in Lid

Spoon

Notebook

Walking Boots

# WHAT ARE MINIBEASTS?

Minibeasts are invertebrates: this means creatures without backbones. Spiders, insects, worms, slugs and snails are all minibeasts.

Snail

Spider

Ant

Worm

Because minibeasts don't have backbones they usually have other **structures** that support and protect them. Snails have shells, and insects and spiders have exoskeletons.

# INSECTS

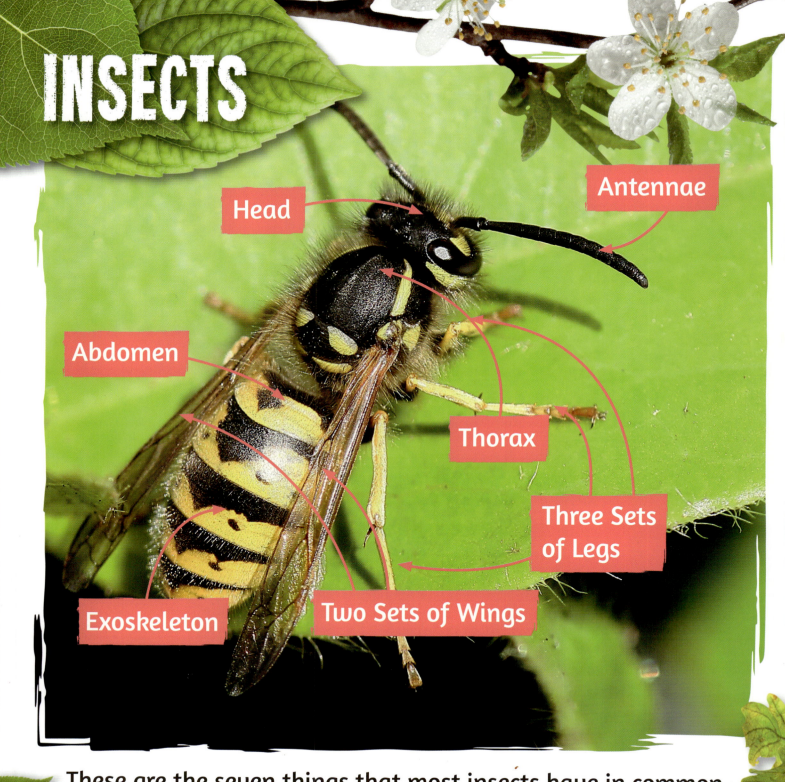

Head

Antennae

Abdomen

Thorax

Three Sets of Legs

Exoskeleton

Two Sets of Wings

These are the seven things that most insects have in common.

Most insects lay eggs. Because exoskeletons don't stretch, insects shed them and grow new ones as they get bigger. You might find an empty exoskeleton.

METAMORPHOSIS: WHEN AN INSECT CHANGES FORM, LIKE A CATERPILLAR INTO A BUTTERFLY

Dragonfly

# WORMS

Worms do not have any arms or legs. Some might have hooks or fins to help them get around, but mostly they are just tubes.

Worms live in the ground where they make tunnels!

Worms eat dead plants and help to keep the soil **fertile**. Lots of forest animals eat worms, such as moles, birds, beetles, frogs and more.

# SNAILS

Snails love to eat leaves. If you are looking for them, look in the trees.

Snails have soft bodies that are protected by a hard shell. The snail can **retract** into the shell.

Snails have eyes at the end of their long tentacles!
The underside of a snail is called the foot.

Shell

Eyes

Tentacles

Mouth

Foot

# SPIDERS

Spiders have eight legs and spin webs. Spiders use their webs to catch **prey**. They mostly eat insects.

**SOME SPIDERS ARE VENOMOUS. LEAVE THEM ALONE AND DON'T TOUCH!**

Spider silk (used to make webs) is one of the strongest materials in the world.

If you are looking for spiders when exploring the forest, keep an eye out for spider webs.

# MINIBEAST HUNT

Try carefully moving a rock to find beetles and bugs!

When looking for minibeasts, it's best to explore dark and damp places. Make sure to carefully replace the rock afterwards.

Places to look for minibeasts:

- Wet soil – this **attracts** worms
- Near water – dragonflies and other insects
- Dark damp areas – snails and slugs love these.

# BE SAFE

Using your spoon, you can pick up minibeasts carefully and place them in your jar to examine.

Make sure that your lid has air holes and is on tightly and safely.

SOME INSECTS CAN BITE. USE YOUR SPOON TO MOVE THEM.

Be careful not to hurt your minibeasts. You are a lot bigger than they are. Always put them back where you found them after examining them.

# EXAMINING MINIBEASTS

Now that you have some minibeasts in your jar,
use your magnifying glass to get a close look.

Can you **identify** which minibeast you have found? Does it have wings? How many legs? Can you see its eyes?

Keep a record of the minibeasts you find.

# KEEPING NOTES

When you do find a minibeast while exploring, it is important to keep careful notes. This way you will be able to identify them later.

Animal: Beetle
Size: Medium
Colour: Green, Shiny
Features: Big Pincers

Animal: Worm
Size: Small
Colour: Pink
Features: Long Body

Note what it looked like and what it was doing.

**Compare** notes with your friends.
See if they have found anything different.

# GLOSSARY

| | |
|---|---|
| **attracts** | pulls or draws towards |
| **compare** | to look at what is the same and what is different between two or more things |
| **exoskeletons** | hard structure on the outside of a creature |
| **fertile** | soil that is able to grow strong, healthy crops |
| **identify** | spot or recognise |
| **prey** | animals that are hunted by other animals for food |
| **retract** | to pull back into |
| **structures** | an organised arrangement |
| **venomous** | capable of injecting venom through a bite or a sting |

# INDEX

24